T0371856

we Garden TOGETHER!

projects for kids:
learn, grow, and
connect with nature

Jane Hirschi
and the Educators at CitySprouts
Photography by Kim Lowe

 Storey Publishing

A GARDEN
is any place where someone is tending and growing things.

Gardens are great for exploring!

Hi There!
We are CitySprouts.

We help schools plant gardens where kids grow plants and learn more about our big, beautiful Earth. At CitySprouts gardens, kids come outside for science lessons and to help take care of the garden. We plant quick-growing greens, flower bulbs, and garlic in the fall. We plant lots of different vegetables and flowers in the spring. Whenever we come out to the garden, we take a look inside the compost bin, too. There's always something interesting to see!

Lots of kids also garden at home. Backyards are one place for a garden, but so are porches and windowsills. Gardening can happen pretty much everywhere—just look around!

With this book, you can try lots of our favorite CitySprouts activities to learn all about how things grow. We hope you have as much fun as we do!

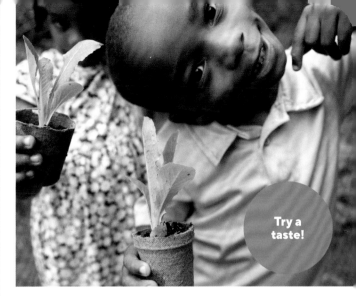

Try a taste!

Learn all about seeds!

Watch things grow!

Contents

Plant

Go on a Seed Hunt 6

Be a Seed Detective 8

Plant a Salad 10

Measure with a Dibble 12

Bucket of Potatoes 14

Grow

Bean in a Bag 16

Grow a Sweet Potato Buddy 18

Garlic Growth Chart 20

Flower Colors 22

Neighborhood Plant Walk 24

Eat

Make Plant Part Art 26

Eat the Rainbow 28

Grow a Kitchen Herb Garden 30

Sprout Snack 32

Discover

Go on a Worm Hunt 34

Make a Worm Bin 36

Make a Snail Terrarium 38

Be a Busy Bee 40

Butterfly Wings! 42

Make a Bird Feeder 44

NOTES FOR PARENTS AND EDUCATORS 46

ACKNOWLEDGMENTS 47

Go on a Seed Hunt

Seeds come in all shapes, colors, and sizes. Let's see how many kinds of seeds we can find in the kitchen! Did you know some spices are seeds, too?

Look at all the shapes and colors!

1 We put all the seeds we found on a plate and mixed them up.

2 We sorted the seeds by color, shape, and size, and put them in an egg carton. Sort your seeds any way you like!

mustard seed

red lentil

fennel seed

soybean

rice

black-eyed pea

cannellini bean

garbanzo bean

corn

brown lentil

black bean

red bean

?

How many different ways can you sort?

Be a Seed Detective

What seeds are hiding inside these fruits and vegetables?

apple cut from top

apple cut from side

pepper

peach

1 We cut open all these fruits and veggies. Look at what's inside!

okra seeds

?
Which have big seeds?
Which have little seeds?

avocado pit

butternut squash seeds

A big seed in the middle of a fruit is called a pit.

What do the seeds feel like?

okra

2 We used spoons and fingers to get the seeds out.

3 Count them! How many seeds can you find in each fruit or vegetable?

Plant a Salad

Lettuce seeds are very small and light. Don't let them blow away! How will they grow and change?

1 First, we filled a cup with potting soil.

Don't bury them too deep! Lettuce seeds need a little light to grow.

2 We sprinkled 5 to 10 tiny lettuce seeds on top of the soil. Then we sprinkled just a little soil on top of them.

3 We watered our seeds gently, just until the soil was damp. Water again whenever the soil dries out!

4 We checked our seeds every day to see how they changed.

? What do you think is happening to the seeds under the soil?

Measure with a Dibble

Dibble is an old-fashioned word for a planting stick. Of course, you can always use your finger to make a hole for the seeds, but it's fun to have a special tool that's decorated just as you like.

1 We used a ½-inch stake to make our dibbles. You can also use a dowel or even a nice straight stick with the bark peeled off.

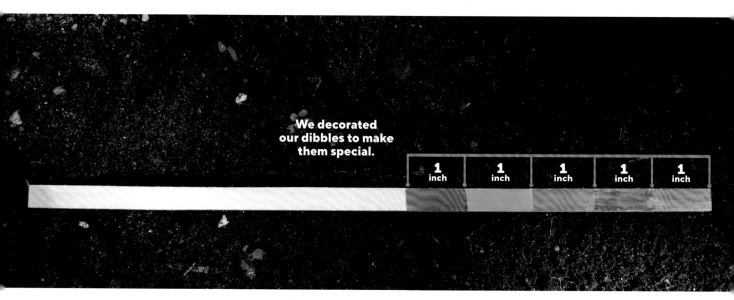

We decorated our dibbles to make them special.

| 1 inch | 1 inch | 1 inch | 1 inch | 1 inch |

2 We used a ruler to make marks 1 inch apart.

?

How deep can you push your dibble into the soil?
How many inch marks are still showing?

3 We pushed our dibble into the soil to make a hole!

4 We planted a zucchini seed 1 inch deep.

5 You can also use your dibble to space your seeds. Check your seed packet to see how deep and how far apart you should plant.

Bucket of Potatoes

Have you ever noticed the "eyes" sprouting on a potato? It's starting to grow! Let's see what happens when we plant a potato.

1 First, we cut a big potato into a few pieces. We let the pieces dry overnight.

Each piece should have an eye or two.

Drill holes in the bottom of the bucket so extra water can drain out.

2 We filled a 5-gallon bucket halfway with soil. We put the potato pieces in and covered them up with another inch of soil. Then we watered them. Water again whenever the soil gets dry.

?

How many potatoes did you find?

3 As the plants grew taller, we added more soil around the stems up to where the leaves were. We kept adding soil to the bucket as our plants grew so that potatoes could form along the stems under the soil.

4 After a few months, when the plants started to turn yellow, our potatoes were ready. Dig down to find your buried treasure!

PLANT

15

Bean in a Bag

What happens to a seed under the soil? We spied on bean seeds germinating (sprouting) in a sandwich bag!

1 First, we wrapped a few bean seeds in a damp paper towel. Garbanzo beans and lentils work well.

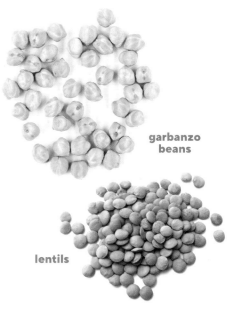

garbanzo beans

lentils

2 Then we put the wrapped seeds in a zip-top baggie and sealed it up!

How has the seed changed since the last time you looked?

3 We opened the baggie and unwrapped the beans every morning and evening so we could peek in to see what they were doing!

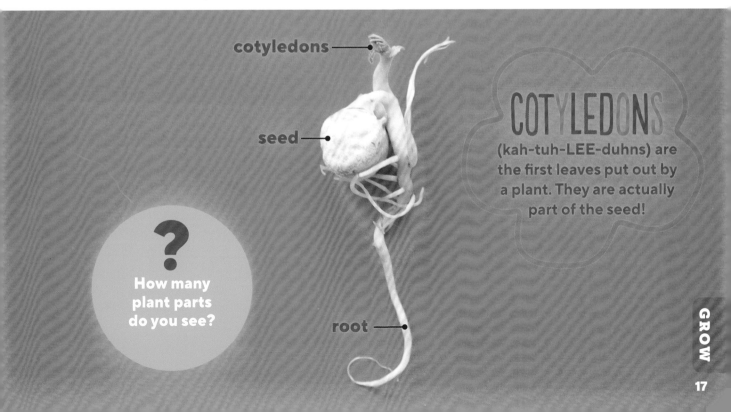

cotyledons

seed

root

How many plant parts do you see?

COTYLEDONS (kah-tuh-LEE-duhns) are the first leaves put out by a plant. They are actually part of the seed!

Grow a Sweet Potato Buddy

Some plants can grow in water! We grew some funny-looking sweet potato plants without using any soil at all.

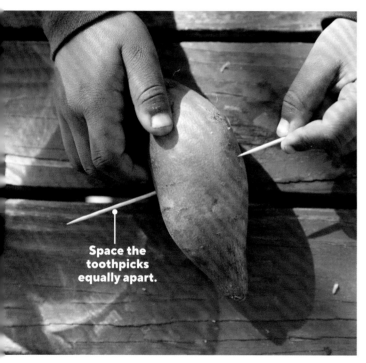

Space the toothpicks equally apart.

1 We poked three toothpicks into the middle of a sweet potato.

2 Then we filled a jar about halfway with water and put the sweet potato in the jar. The end should just barely be touching the water.

? What are the first signs you see that the sweet potato is growing?

This end down! The root end is usually pointier.

Those sprouts look kind of like funny hair!

We drew silly faces on our potatoes.

?

How does your sweet potato change as it grows?

3 We left our sweet potato on a sunny windowsill. After a few weeks it started to grow. Make sure to add water to the jar when it gets low!

Garlic Growth Chart

Garlic can grow in water, too! We measured how long the roots and stem grew every day so we could see how fast it grows.

1 We poked three toothpicks into the middle of a single clove of garlic.

The pointy end of the clove is the top!

Make sure the bottom of the garlic touches the water.

2 Then we filled a jar with water and placed the garlic in the jar.

? What does garlic smell like?

?

Where do you first see the garlic clove changing?

3 We put the jar on a sunny windowsill. Make sure to add water to the jar when it gets low!

4 Every few days we took the garlic clove out of the jar to measure it on a piece of paper.

FRIDAY, MAY 13

WEDNESDAY, MAY 11

TUESDAY, MAY 10
MONDAY, MAY 9
START   TUESDAY, MAY 3

?

How much did your garlic grow in a week?

START   TUESDAY, MAY 3
SATURDAY, MAY 7
MONDAY, MAY 9

TUESDAY, MAY 10

WEDNESDAY, MAY 11

FRIDAY, MAY 13

GROW

Flower Colors

Flowers are so pretty! They're important, too, because they are how a plant makes fruit and seeds so that more plants can grow. We took a walk to see how many different flower colors we could find.

1 We found white and blue flowers along the roadside and yellow flowers in the park!

2 We took a few flowers home and put them in water.

Look, a bee! Bees and other pollinators like the flower's bright colors.

3 We used tissue paper to make all the different-colored flowers we saw. Choose some tissue paper that matches your flower. Then tear or scrunch up pieces and glue them to construction paper.

? How many different colors did you find? How many shapes?

4 Whenever we see a new flower, we make a new tissue-paper flower to match it!

Neighborhood Plant Walk

Plants are growing all around us! We went on a plant walk and found them growing in many different places.

Ivy is growing on this building.

Trees are plants, too.

Plants can even grow right through cracks in the pavement!

1 We found lots of different kinds of plants on just a short walk. They come in all different shapes and sizes!

? What sizes and shapes of leaves did you find on your plant walk?

? What were the tallest and smallest plants you found?

? What plants with flowers did you see?

2 We took some photos of the plants we saw on our walk.

3 Later, we drew and painted pictures of them!

Make Plant Part Art

People eat lots of different plants. Sometimes we eat the leaves, sometimes we eat the stems, and sometimes we eat the roots! We made cool designs with edible plants and then tasted our art.

leaves

fruit

flowers

roots

stems

1 We used all these different plants to make our designs!
Can you find the plants with roots to eat? And stems to eat?

Do you want a bite?

?

Can you think of other plants you like to eat?

2 Look at our beautiful plates! Take a photo or draw a picture of your creation before you start munching.

3 We tasted our designs. Yum! Which plants are tastiest to you?

EAT

Eat the Rainbow

Fruits and veggies come in so many different colors! If we eat all the colors, we know we're getting lots of healthy nutrients for our bodies.

We tasted every **color!**

1 We searched our kitchen and the market for all different colors of fruits and vegetables. See what we found!

2 We laid out pieces of colored paper and matched our fruits and veggies to each color.

?

Which color in your rainbow has the most fruits and veggies?

3 Look at our delicious rainbow! Taste every color. Which colors taste the best to you?

EAT

Grow a Kitchen Herb Garden

We grew a little garden on the windowsill! It smells good and tastes good, too. Most plants come in small pots they quickly outgrow. Here's how we transplanted our herbs to give them room to stretch their roots.

1 We started with three different kinds of potted herbs that we got from the grocery store.

2 We tipped each pot and gently pulled the plants out, soil and all.

? Gently rub the leaves with your fingers. What do they smell like?

3 We filled a planter with soil and used our hands to scoop out a space for each herb.

4 We put the plants in and covered the roots. We gently pressed the soil down around the stems to remove any air pockets. Make sure to water your plants when the soil gets dry!

? Herbs are all different shapes and sizes. Do they taste different, too?

Sprout Snack

We grew sprouts in a jar. In just a few days, they were big enough to snack on! Alfalfa, mung, or broccoli seeds all make great sprouts.

1 We put seeds in a quart-size jar—just enough to cover the bottom.

2 We covered them with water and let them soak overnight.

3 We covered the top of the jar with two layers of cheesecloth so air could pass in and out. We used a rubber band to hold it on.

4 In the morning, we drained the sprouts through the cheesecloth. Then we rinsed them by pouring a couple cups of water through the cheesecloth and pouring it out again, right through the cloth.

Pat the top of the cloth to free any seeds that are stuck there.

?

What changes do you see in the seeds as they grow?

5 We rinsed and drained our sprouts twice a day, morning and evening. This is important because it keeps them safe to eat!

6 In just a few days, our sprouts were ready to eat! Be sure to rinse them again before eating or refrigerating. How do they taste to you?

EAT

Go on a Worm Hunt

Worms are wiggly and wonderful! They keep gardens healthy by making tunnels in the soil so air can get in. They eat dead plants and leave behind their nutrient-rich castings (poop) to help new plants grow.

We found them in the grass.

We found them on the sidewalk after it rained.

1 We walked around our city block and looked for places where worms might live.

We found them in the community garden.

2 We picked one up. Be gentle! Remember that worms are living things.

3 Time to take a closer look! Where are the worm's head and tail? Watch how a worm uses its whole body to move!

clitellum, where eggs are stored

tail

head

? Can you wiggle like a worm?

Make a Worm Bin

We made a worm bin so we could watch how worms work. They turned our paper and fruit scraps into soil!

1 We found three or four worms in the garden for starting our worm bin.

Make the strips no more than 1 inch wide. You can also use a shredder.

2 We filled a shoebox-size plastic container halfway with newspaper strips.

3 The newspaper should be damp. We used a spray bottle, but you can also sprinkle water by hand.

4 The worms are in their new home! We added a handful of soil and a few apple peels and covered the box with a lid. Be sure to make holes in the lid so the worms can breathe.

?

What happens to the food you put in your worm bin?

5 Check on your worm bin every few days. Once every week or two, add another small piece of fruit or vegetable such as a lettuce leaf or carrot.

Make a Snail Terrarium

Snails carry their homes on their backs! We found snails in the park. You might find them on the sidewalk or around plants after it rains.

1 We collected a few snails in a jar and brought them inside for a closer look. Cover the jar opening with thin cloth secured with a rubber band so that air can get in.

2 We watched the snails as they moved. You can put them on a paper plate and look at them closely with a magnifying glass!

? Notice how snails move their bodies. Can you move your body like a snail?

3 Remember to take the snails back to where you found them (or a similar place) when you are finished observing them.

Be a Busy Bee

When flowers are blooming, we see bees everywhere. Do you see bees in your neighborhood?

This bee is pollinating a flower!

1 We saw bees in the garden. We also heard them buzzing in the weeds by the side of the road!

You can also attach pom-poms with hot glue!

2 Twist two pipe cleaners together to make a headband, and tie on two more so they stick straight up. Now you have antennae just like a bee!

3 Let's pretend to be bees! Outside, we can visit flowers like the bees do. If you are indoors, you can create an imaginary garden by pretending the furniture are flowers.

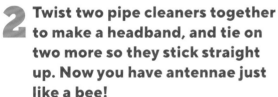

Notice how bees move.

Can you buzz around like a bee?

Butterfly Wings!

Beautiful butterflies are fun to watch. We made wings and fluttered like butterflies!

Butterflies pollinate flowers, too!

1 First, we cut out two pie-shaped pieces from a paper plate to make the shape of a butterfly's wings.

2 We decorated our wings to make them colorful like a butterfly's!

3 We wrapped a pipe cleaner around the middle to make the butterfly's antennae.

4 We took our butterflies outside to fly! If you are indoors, you can create an imaginary garden for your butterflies to fly in.

?

Do you see butterflies in your neighborhood? Where?

Make a Bird Feeder

Birds come to our garden looking for seeds, insects, and worms to eat. We made a bird feeder so we could get a closer look at who comes to visit!

Start cutting about 2 inches from the bottom of the carton.

1 First, we cut a rectangle in the side of a half-gallon milk carton.

2 Then we punched a hole at the top of the carton so we could loop a string or wire through.

You can make a perch with a pencil or chopstick. Just punch a hole and push the stick through.

3 Use acrylic paint or waterproof markers to decorate your feeder. Fill the bottom of the carton with birdseed from the store.

What's a good place for a bird feeder? Try the side of your porch, in a tree, outside a window, or some other place high enough to keep other animals from eating the food.

4 Keep an eye on your bird feeder. What kinds of birds are coming to visit?

Cardinal

Chickadee

Experiment with different kinds of birdseed and see who shows up!

?

Where else do you see birds in your neighborhood?

Robin

Notes for Parents and Educators

Growing plants in a garden and watching plants grow in nature is a terrific way for children and adults alike to learn more about the natural world. Observing plants as they grow prompts big questions:

- *What is alive and what is not alive?*

- *What do living things need to grow and thrive?*

- *How do living things change over time?*

- *How are plants and animals, including people, dependent on each other?*

The activities in this book encourage preschoolers to wonder, to ask questions, to think, and to talk about some of the most important big ideas at the foundation of the life sciences. They encourage children and grown-ups to use their senses to learn more about the world: to observe, smell, touch, and sometimes taste. Gardening with preschoolers is fun and immensely rewarding.

Their wonder and curiosity is infectious! Growing together can set your preschooler on a lifelong path of deep interest in and appreciation for the natural world we live in.

Adults can support preschoolers on this journey. Notice when and how they are expressing wonder or asking questions about what they sense. Encourage their curiosity. Each activity includes questions meant to encourage children and grown-ups alike to observe more closely, to make predictions, and to express what they are thinking. Adults encourage children when they share their wondering out loud and invite children to likewise share. (It's okay, too, if a child chooses not to speak; the invitation alone can prompt deeper thinking.)

Giving preschoolers opportunities to wonder, explore, and predict on their own is an important step in the process of deep learning. The following are some of the big life science ideas in this book's activities. Listen and look for signs that your preschooler is wondering about these big ideas.

Basic Characteristics of Living Things

All living things—plants and animals—have basic needs such as nutrients, water, and air. Living things also have different parts that serve different functions and help them live and grow. A plant's stem, for instance, helps it get water from its roots to its leaves. Many kinds of animals use their mouths to get water into their bodies. There are different kinds of plants and animals. Even animals of the same kind have differences (variation), though, just as people do.

Changes Over Time

Living things change over time and grow in a sequence called a life cycle. The seed begins to change as soon as it germinates. The plant continues to change throughout its life cycle. People and other animals change throughout their life cycles, too. Plants and animals come in all sizes and shapes, from a pea sprout to an oak tree and from an ant to an elephant. All living things are changing constantly (but at very different rates). Preschoolers along with adults can observe evidence of change. What signs of change in living things is your preschooler noticing?

Interconnectedness

Living things depend on elements of their environment that are not living such as sunlight, rain, and soil. They also depend on other living things. Bean vines growing in the garden, for instance, "climb" up sunflower stems to grow higher toward the sun. Worms and other soil creatures burrow down in the soil to avoid the sun and to find things to eat. Bees collect pollen from flowering plants. Plants growing outside depend on worms to add nutrients to the soil and on bees to pollinate their flowers. Plants also help people and other animals grow and thrive. They provide us with healthy and nutritious food and add oxygen to the air we breathe. Plants of all kinds help cool our planet.

Using Our Senses to Learn

Our senses help us learn about the world around us. We use our eyes to observe how plants and animals are similar to and different from each other. Our sense of smell often gives us information about what is good to eat. Our sense of touch tells us about characteristics of different plants—leaves can be soft and fuzzy or shiny and smooth, for example. Ask your preschooler to describe what they see, touch, or smell. Putting words to experience is an important learning skill.

ACKNOWLEDGMENTS

Every book starts with the seed of an idea. Thank you to Hannah Fries and Deanna Cook for recognizing a great idea and partnering with CitySprouts to help it grow into this book. Thanks to Carolyn Eckert for her artistic vision and her down-to-earth appreciation for how children see the world. We are grateful to Storey Publishing for helping us bring CitySprouts' garden activities into families' homes.

Enormous appreciation goes to photographer Kim Lowe, whose images in this book are but a sampling of the many amazing photographs she's taken of CitySprouts over the years. Few can match Kim's energy, skill, and passion to share the joy of children exploring nature.

For more than 20 years, CitySprouts has been partnering with teachers in dozens of city schoolyards to nurture children's natural curiosity and wonder. Appreciations go to the Garden Educators who developed these activities over the years, especially our Garden Educators today: Sydney, Melissa, Kathryn, Karl, Heather, and Degen. Hats off as well to the people who make the Garden Educators' work possible: Therecia, Solomon, Jessica, Jane, and Avalon.

CitySprouts is indebted to Karen Worth and Jeff Winokur for sharing their immense knowledge and experience of elementary science, guiding CitySprouts toward ever deeper science learning.

Most of all, heartfelt thanks go to the thousands of children who've learned from and loved their CitySprouts school gardens. This book is dedicated to them and their families, in the hope and expectation that every child will come to know the joy and excitement of living, growing things.

Jane Hirschi
Executive Director, CitySprouts

The mission of Storey Publishing is to serve our customers by publishing practical information that encourages personal independence in harmony with the environment.

EDITED BY Deanna F. Cook and Hannah Fries

ART DIRECTION AND BOOK DESIGN BY Carolyn Eckert

TEXT PRODUCTION BY Jennifer Jepson Smith

COVER AND INTERIOR PHOTOGRAPHY BY © Kim Lowe Photography, www.kimlowe.com, except Mars Vilaubi © Storey Publishing, LLC, front (b.r.) and back (t.r.)

ADDITIONAL PHOTOGRAPHY BY © AlasdairJames/iStock.com, 8 b.l.; © Andreas Häuslbetz/iStock.com, 24 b.r.; © Art Sublimina Photography/iStock.com, 45 (cardinal); © blickwinkel/Alamy Stock Photo, 35 b.r.; © BrianEKushner/iStock.com, 45 (chickadee); Carolyn Eckert © Storey Publishing, LLC, 21; CE © Storey Publishing, LLC, 25 b.r.; © Creativeye99/iStock.com, 8 2nd f.b.l.; © Eddie Pearson/Stocksy, 22 t.l.; © eyewave/iStock.com, 8 b.c.; © Floortje/iStock.com, 8 b.r.; © HamidEbrahimi/iStock.com, 45 (robin); Hannah Fries © Storey Publishing, LLC, 23 b.r.; © jimplumb/iStock.com, 25 b.l.; © Linda Raymond/iStock.com, 22 t.r.; Marisol Benitez/Unsplash, 28 (vegetables); Mars Vilaubi © Storey Publishing, LLC, 12 t. & m.r., 19, 23 b.l., 27 r. (all), 32 t.l., 42 b., 44 t.r., 48 2nd f.t.; © mustafa güner/iStock.com, 16 t.r.; © Pansfun Images/Stocksy, 30b.; © racheldonahue/iStock.com, 16 b.r.; © scorpion56/iStock.com, 34 t.l.

COVER AND INTERIOR ILLUSTRATIONS BY Carolyn Eckert © Storey Publishing, LLC, except front cover and throughout (butterflies), 4 and throughout (three beans), 6 (red bean), 20, 27, 28, and 47 by Ilona Sherratt © Storey Publishing, LLC

TEXT © 2023 BY CITYSPROUTS

The information in this book is true and complete to the best of our knowledge. All recommendations are made without guarantee on the part of the author or Storey Publishing. The author and publisher disclaim any liability in connection with the use of this information.

Storey books are available at special discounts when purchased in bulk for premiums and sales promotions as well as for fundraising or educational use. Special editions or book excerpts can also be created to specification. For details, please call 800-827-8673, or send an email to sales@storey.com.

Storey Publishing
210 MASS MoCA Way
North Adams, MA 01247
storey.com

Printed in China by Shenzhen Reliance Printing Co. Ltd.
10 9 8 7 6 5 4 3 2 1

Library of Congress Cataloging-in-Publication Data on file